# RISK-TAKING AND DECISION-MAKING:

## HOW TO STACK THE ODDS IN YOUR FAVOR

by: BILL TREASURER, FOUNDER, GIANT LEAP CONSULTING, INC.

LITTLE LEAPS
PRESS

# OBJECTIVES

- Evaluate the nature of risk
- Define the importance of risk and performance
- Learn the protective frame
- **RISKING RIGHT**
- Understand the 5 P's of Risk Taking
- Learn how to evaluate risk
- Discuss the most common approaches for managing risk

# DEAR READER,

Kudos to you for purchasing this resource! If you're like most people, you could stand to take more personal and business risks. Of course, you'll want to do that in a thoughtful and calculated way so as to reduce the likelihood of getting harmed. The good news is, this resource is designed to help you do just that: **help you take risks more thoughtfully and decisively while reducing the chance of wiping out.**

To be clear, I'm a risk-taker. I am a former Captain of the U.S. High Diving Team and performed over 1500 dives from heights that scaled to over 100 feet, traveling at speeds in excess of 50 mph, and then hitting a small pool that was only 10 feet deep. To make things more absurd, many of those dives were performed while *on fire!* As part of our aquatic entertainment production, our evening high diving show would culminate with a visit from Captain Inferno who would light his gasoline-saturated cape and become engulfed in flames before diving into the pool below.

Don't believe me? The cover of my first book, *Right Risk: Ten Powerful Principles for Taking Giant Leaps With Your Life*, has a picture of me on fire in front of 2000 startled spectators.

After retiring my Speedo™, I took up whitewater kayaking. My river-rat friends and I would splash down the boulderous rivers of the Southeast, navigating intimidatingly-named rapids like *table saw, witch's hole, and decapitation rock.*

Bear in mind that as much as I'm a risk-taker, I'm also a big scaredy cat. Strangely, it's not the fact that I am a risk-taker that qualified me to write this material. It's the fact that I take risks *when I'm afraid.* I built my entire business around this concept. Getting out into your discomfort zone, by facing challenges that are hard and scary is how you build your courage. **Courage—which I see as risk-taking in action—isn't fear*less*. It's fear*ful!*** When you face a big consequential decision, or when you make a big bold work move, you are full of knee-knocking, teeth-chattering, palm-sweating fear...but if you persist despite those fears, you're being courageous.

Two decades ago I quit a six-figure job to strike out on my own and founded Giant Leap Consulting as the world's first courage-building company. Since then my company has taught courage-building workshops to thousands of leaders and employees in twelve countries on five continents. Much of the material here is drawn from that work.

As you immerse yourself in this material, my greatest hope for you is that you'll play it less safe in life and at work so that you can live in a bigger, bolder, louder, and more courageous way!

Be Courageous!

**BILL TREASURER**
Founder, Giant Leap Consulting, Inc.
*(GiantLeapConsulting.com)*

# " "

# THAT WHICH IS CLEARLY KNOWN HATH LESS TERROR THAN THAT WHICH IS HINTED AND GUESSED AT.

— ARTHUR CONAN DOYLE
*Author and creator of the character Sherlock Holmes*

# THE NATURE OF RISK:
## PERCEPTION & REALITY

There are two types of risk: real risk and perceived risk. Real risks involve probability and likelihood. Perceived risk is largely impacted and distorted by human perception. Below are just a few of the ways that the perception of risk gets twisted by human nature.

## PERCEIVED RISKS

### THE NEWER THE RISK, THE MORE FEAR IT INSPIRES:
People are more afraid of new risks than ones they've known about for a while. When HIV AIDS was discovered during the 1980s, people viewed it as a new Black Plague. Today it is viewed with much less fear as a largely treatable sexually transmitted disease.

### UNNATURAL RISKS ARE VIEWED AS MORE DANGEROUS:
People have more concerns about radiation exposure from cell phones than radiation exposure from the sun, which is far more dangerous and likely.

### RISKS YOU HAVE NO CHOICE OVER ARE SCARIER:
People are more afraid of risks that they have little choice about facing. Many smokers, for example, worry more about asbestos exposure at work than the impact of their own smoking on their health.

### RISKS YOU HAVE NO CONTROL OVER ARE SCARIER:
People view flying in a commercial airplane as more dangerous than driving their own car...despite the fact that the chances of dying in a vehicle death are far greater.

### RISK THAT CAN KILL YOU IN AWFUL WAYS ARE VIEWED AS SCARIER:
People are more afraid of getting attacked and killed by a shark than by dying of heart disease...something that is far more likely.

# " THE MORE SEVERE THE OUTCOME, THE HIGHER WE JUDGE THE RISK TO BE.

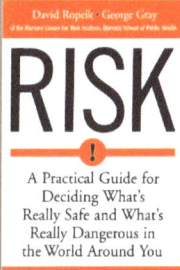

— DAVID ROPEIK AND GEORGE GRAY
*Risk: A Practical Guide for Deciding What's Really Safe and What's Really Dangerous in the World Around You*

# THE NATURE OF RISK:
## PERCEPTION & REALITY

## EXAMPLES:

### HEART DISEASE
Heart disease is the leading killer in the U.S. Out of every 100 deaths, 34 are from heart disease. About 700,000 U.S. deaths each year.

### MOTOR VEHICLES
Motor vehicle accidents are the leading cause of death for the population of people between 1 and 38 years old.

### FALLS
Falls are the most common cause of accidental death in the U.S. Each year 1 out of every 3 older adults (65 or older) falls and suffers some sort of injury.

### DROWNING
Drowning is the leading cause of accidental death for children between ages 1 and 4. Most die in backyard swimming pools and 5X more males drown than females.

### FIRES
The U.S. has the highest death rate from fires than any other industrialized nation Cooking is the leading cause of house fires, but smoking is the leading cause of home fire deaths.

### CANCER
1 out of every 2 U.S. males will get some form of cancer in their lives. 1 out of every 3 U.S. women will too. Cancer kills, on average, a half million people every year. There are over 100 types of cancer, 4 are responsible for over 50% of all cancer deaths (lung, colorectal, breast, and prostate).

Source: *Risk: A Practical Guide for Deciding What's Really Safe and What's Really Dangerous in the World Around You*, by David Ropeik and George Gray

# YEARLY 💀 ODDS

**1 in 80,089,128**
Winning the U.S.
Powerball lottery

**1 in 280,000,000**
Dying in a shark attack

**1 in 140,000,000**
Dying in an alligator attack

**1 in 94,000,000**
Dying in a bear attack

**1 IN 59,000,000**
Dying in a high school
football game

**1 in 9,100,000**
Dying while skydiving

**1 in 3,000,000**
Dying from a strike
of lightening

**1 in 840,000**
Drowning in your bathtub

**1 in 18,000**
Dying due to a gunshot

**1 in 300**
Dying of heart disease

Source: *Risk: A Practical Guide for Deciding What's Really Safe and What's Really Dangerous in the World Around You,* by David Ropeik and George Gray

# RISK & PERFORMANCE:
## THE IMPORTANCE OF AROUSAL

In 1908 two American psychologists, Robert Yerkes and J.D. Dodson, began researching the relationship between arousal and peak performance. Their work resulted in the establishment of the Yerkes-Dotson Law. The law suggests that performance increases with mental and physiological arousal...but only up to a point. But after reaching a certain threshold, arousal (such as that caused by anxiety/fear) has diminishing performance returns.

The upward part of the curve below can be thought of as energy-producing, while the downward part of the curve can be thought of as energy-sapping (e.g., stress). Facing a personal risk, one needs to consider the severity of the potential outcomes, and the likelihood of that outcome occurring.

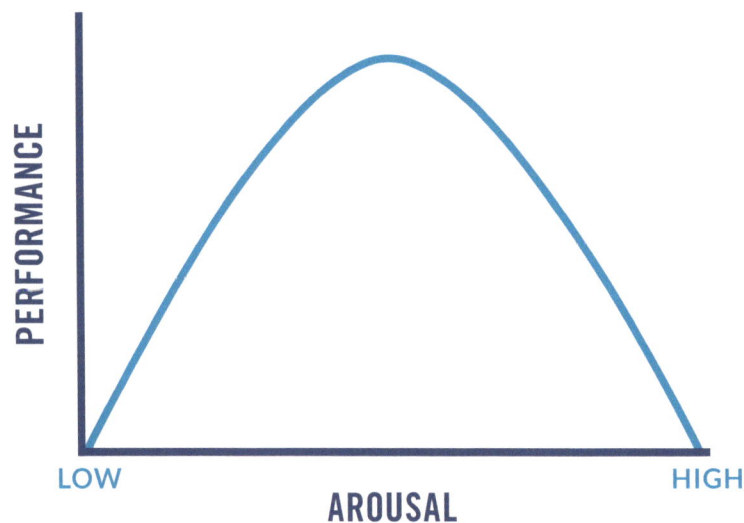

## THE THRESHOLD AT WHICH AROUSAL BEGINS TO HAVE DIMINISHING RETURNS IS UNIQUE TO EACH INDIVIDUAL.

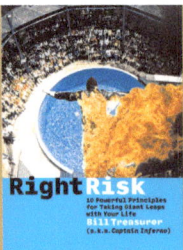

"To live is to risk; to risk it to live."
—*Bill Treasurer*

# THE RISKS YOU REGRET THE MOST ARE THE ONES YOU DIDN'T TAKE.

— BILL TREASURER
*Author of* Risking Right

# AROUSAL & PROTECTION

Michael J. Apter wrote The Dangerous Edge: The Psychology of Excitement (Free Press, 1992) which challenges the Yerkes / Dotson model by arguing that human beings can withstand tremendous amounts of arousal without diminishing performance as long as they have a robust "protective frame."

## FEAR AND EXCITEMENT

Fear and excitement are "neurological correlates"—meaning, your body experiences the same physiological responses to intense feelings of fear (e.g., fast heartbeat, sweating, dilated eyes, etc.) as intense feelings of excitement.

The only real difference between fear and excitement is that we experience fear as displeasure and we experience excitement as pleasure. Having a strong protective frame helps us shift over from fear to excitement, moving us toward the risk instead of away from hit.

The more our confidence grows, the more safe we feel, and the more willing we are to take risks. This is true whether you are learning to ride a bike, making one more sales call in the face of rejection, or dealing with a new company performance management system.

## APTER ON THE "PROTECTIVE FRAME."

"Think of looking at a tiger in a cage. *Both* the tiger and the cage are needed in order to experience excitement: The tiger without the cage would be frightening; the cage without the tiger would be boring. Both are necessary. In order to experience excitement, then, we need both the possibility of danger and something we believe will protect us from it."

## THE BOTTOM LINE

When feeling intense feelings of negative arousal (i.e., fear), instead of focusing reducing the fear, focus on taking the actions that will build your confidence.

**AROUSAL** ⬇

**PROTECTION** ⬇

**BORING** =

**AROUSAL** ⬆

**PROTECTION** ⬇

**FRIGHTENING** =

**AROUSAL** ⬆

**PROTECTION** ⬆

**EXCITING** =

# AROUSAL & PROTECTION:
## REFLECTIVE EVALUATION

**WHAT RISK ARE YOU NOW FACING IS PROMPTING A LOT OF FEAR?**

**WHAT ARE YOU MOST AFRAID OF RELATIVE TO THIS RISK?** *What factual data do you have that supports your being afraid?*

**ON A SCALE OF 1 TO 10,** *with 1 equating with "my protective frame is weak" and 10 equating with "my protective frame is strong," how strong is your protective frame as it relates to the risk you are considering?*

**WHAT SPECIFIC ACTIONS COULD YOU TAKE TO BUILD YOUR CONFIDENCE** *and strengthen your protective frame in order to help you take this risk?*

# RISK EVALUATION:
## BALANCING SEVERITY & LIKELIHOOD

When facing a personal risk, one needs to consider the severity of the potential outcomes, and the likelihood of that outcome occurring. The Worst Case Grid (below) will help you evaluate your risk.

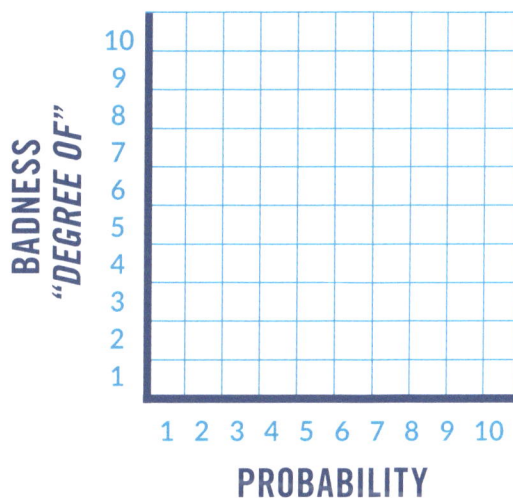

On a scale ranging between 1 and 10, rate how catastrophic (i.e., how "bad") it would be if the change were an abysmal failure. Next, rate the probability of this outcome occurring. Now multiply the two figures.

$$B \times P = \underline{\hspace{2cm}}$$

While even a change with a score in the 90s can sometimes be worth taking, generally you are safest when your scores under 50. However, the decision to change is based on your tolerance for risk. Thus the critical question is: Is the score acceptable to you?!

Keep in mind that the grid is a perception-based tool. It's only as good as your instincts!

*Of course it's also good to assess your upside potential. You can create a Best Case Grid by rating the degree of "goodness" instead of badness.*

© LITTLE LEAPS PRESS, INC. ALL RIGHTS RESERVED.                    14

# THE 5 P'S OF RISKTAKING

## PASSION:

By arousing the strongest, most untamed parts of our nature, and stirring up the wild mustangs in our soul, our passion gives us the raw energy and wherewithal to suffer through the anguishing moments that often accompany right risk.

## PURPOSE:

Purpose serves to harness our passions and give them direction. Ask, "How will this risk make me a more complete person? How will this risk further my life's purpose? How will it help me get to where I want to go?"

## PRINCIPLE:

Right Risks are governed by a set of values that are both essential and virtuous. As mentioned, risks are essentially decisions, and when facing a decision of consequences, principles form a set of criteria against which the risk can be judged.

## PREROGATIVE:

Right-risk takers view the power to choose as a privilege, and then honor it as such. By consistently making choices at a conscious level, they are better able to make superior judgment calls at an instinctual level—in fast-moving situations.

## PROFIT:

A Right Risk should come with a real potential for gain. Risks are, well, risky. And in exchange for assuming the potential risk of hardship, you are entitled to some real and unequivocal upside Notice, however, that Profit is the fifth "P". It's the criteria that should be assessed last.

**"I'd rather regret the things I have done than the things I haven't."**
—*Lucille Ball*

# THE 5 P'S OF RISKTAKING:
## REFLECTIVE EVALUATION

**PASSION:** *When you consider this risk, does it give you energy or zap it? How passionate are you about this risk?*

**PURPOSE:** *What higher-order purpose is this risk connected to? How will taking the risk move you to your goals? How will it help close the gap between the person you are and the person you're aiming to become?*

**PRINCIPLE:** *What deeply held principles will taking this risk uphold? Will taking it be a demonstration of your faith? Independence? Courage? Something else?*

**PREROGATIVE:** *Will taking this risk be an exercise of your own free will, or do you feel forced into it by someone else? The most successful risks are those of our own taking!*

**PROFIT:** *What do you stand to gain if the risk is successful? How important is this potential gain to you?*

## OTHER FACTORS TO CONSIDER WHEN FACING A RISK:

- **Downside & probability:** What could go wrong and how likely is it that it will?
- **Upside & probability:** What could go right and how likely is it that it will?
- **Controllable & uncontrollable factors:** What important factors can you control? What important factors are beyond your control?
- **Reversibility:** If you make a decision and it starts to go bad, how reversible is it?
- **Contingency plans:** What plans can you put in place upfront so you can act quickly if the decision goes south?
- **Early indicators:** What are some early "red flag" indicators that the decision needs to be reconsidered?

# EXPERT RISK-TAKING ADVICE

### ASK FOR FEEDBACK!

Ask a trusted friend at work to rate you 1-10 (10 is perfect) on some skill (e.g. speaking, negotiating) and then to tell you what you'd be doing more of or less of if you were a 10. Now you know what to try!

#### SHARON JORDAN-EVANS

*President of the Jordan Evans Group, and author of* Love 'Em or Lose 'Em.
*www.jeg.org*

### COURAGE!

We need courage when we experience fear. A starting point to access the needed courage is to sit with the fear. What is this fear really about? When fear remains generalized it paralyzes. When it is examined, plumbed, named and seen as it really is, it becomes smaller than us. We can then tap into the energy it contains and channel that energy towards accomplishing whatever difficult task we are called to do.

#### IRA CHALEFF

*Author,* The Courageous Follower: Standing Up To and For Our Leaders.
*www.courageousfollower.net*

### FIND A CAUSE!

We only 'find' courage when we find something to fight for a cause, a dream, a project, a person, a group less fortunate than ourselves. We tap into our deepest strengths and reserves not when we act with self-interest but rather when we are lost in the fight for something larger than ourselves."

#### BRENDON BURCHARD

*Author of* Life's Golden Ticket. *www.lifesgoldenticket.com*

## BE DEFIANT!

Chuck House, a maverick engineer at HP, once said, "Come to work each day willing to be fired." He came up with a breakthrough idea for HP they eventually made gobs of money on, but at the time even the founders tried to kill. Once Chuck's idea proved to be successful, HP created the Chuck House Medal of Defiance. Chuck House was the first recipient.

### ROBERT B. TUCKER

*Corporate Innovation Guru and author of* Driving Growth Through Innovation. *www.innovationresource.com*

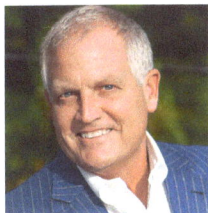

## BEGIN BEFORE BEGINNING!

I instruct executives to approach a risk by beginning before the beginning. Research your family history and identify the relatives that you consider to be courageous. After only brief look back into your family history, you'll probably find a courageous immigrant who left the safe shores of their homeland to come to America. When facing a risk, what advice do you think your courageous relatives would give you?

### BILL TREASURER

*Chief Encouragement Officer, Giant Leap Consulting. Author of* Courageous Leadership. *www.couragebuilding.com*

"

# FEAR IS LIKE FIRE. IT CAN COOK FOR YOU. IT CAN HEAT YOUR HOUSE OR IT CAN BURN IT DOWN.

— CUS D'AMATO
*Famed boxing trainer of Mike Tyson, Floyd Patterson, and José Torres.*

# RE-WRITE YOUR RISK SCRIPTS

Each individual grows up with a lot of "scripting" from his or her parents. It can range from "You're so smart and handsome" to "You'll never amount to anything." Over time, we develop a psychological narrative that we begin bend our lives toward. How we approach risks and decisions is also impacted by our scripting and the stories we tell ourselves.

*What follows are some of the more common limiting scripts, first introduced in the book, Right Risk, by Giant Leap's founder, Bill Treasurer. The third column provides alternative scripts that can be mentally recited when you need to overcome a negative risk script.*

| LIMITING RISK SCRIPT | CONSEQUENCES | ALTERNATIVE MANTRAS |
|---|---|---|
| **I am not enough.** | • Strong feelings of inadequacy<br>• Perfectionism<br>• Hyper-ambitious, endlessly "proving" your worthiness to yourself | • I am enough<br>• Calm Confidence<br>• Enough Already |
| **I must always be in control.** | • Hyper-focus on risk-mitigation<br>• Dominating, dogmatic, and overcontrolling<br>• Personal rigidity / lack of spontaneity<br>• Joyless | • It's not about me<br>• Doing right beats being right<br>• Ask, don't tell<br>• Let go |
| **People always let you down.** | • Unrealistically low expectations of others<br>• People are presumed guilty from the start<br>• Emotionally distant, lonely<br>• Suspicious of other's motives / distrusting | • People are doing the best they can<br>• They are like me<br>• Maybe it's me |
| **I am better than you.** | • Annoyance when your way isn't selected<br>• Dismissive of the ideas of others<br>• Shallow, justifying "better" according to income level, organizational rank, etc. | • I am just like you<br>• Everyone leaves the same way<br>• Get humble fast<br>• Values matter most |

# RE-WRITE YOUR RISK SCRIPTS

## OTHER USEFUL MANTRAS

| | | |
|---|---|---|
| NO RISK, NO REWARD | GET OVER YOURSELF! | INSIST ON YOURSELF! |
| LET GO | HOLD ON | FOCUS! |
| PERSONAL FIDELITY | FOLLOW YOUR BLISS | STAY IN THE MOMENT |
| NO BOUNDARIES | KNOW BOUNDARIES | IT'S ALL GOOD! |
| KEEP THE FAITH | TRUST GOD | CARPE DIEM! |

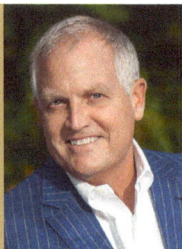

"My mantra helped me coach more assertively and be more self-respectful; I will fear no person on Earth. I got the mantra after hearing a recording of Martin Luther King, Jr., where he said 'Tonight I am fearing no man.' He was quoting Mahatma Gandhi."
—Bill Treasurer, *author*, Right Risk

RE-WRITE YOUR RISK SCRIPTS

# RE-WRITE YOUR RISK SCRIPTS:
## REFLECTIVE EVALUATION

WHAT IS A LIMITING RISK SCRIPT THAT YOU MAY HAVE BEEN INFLUENCED BY?

WHAT CONSEQUENCES HAVE YOU EXPERIENCED BY FOLLOWING YOUR LIMITING RISK SCRIPT?

WHAT IS A HEALTHY REFRAMING—A "MANTRA"—YOU COULD USE TO BE MORE POSITIVE ABOUT YOUR RISK? *Feel free to use one that was included on the prior page!*

© LITTLE LEAPS PRESS, INC.  ALL RIGHTS RESERVED.

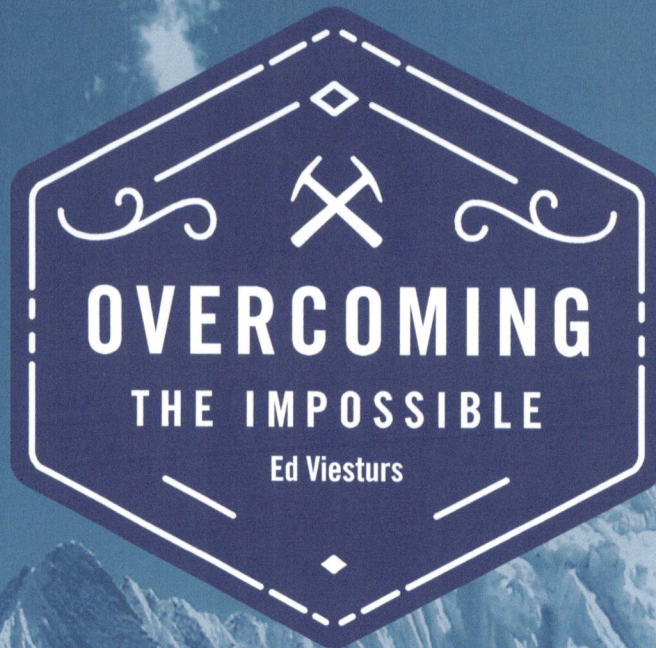

# OVERCOMING
## THE IMPOSSIBLE
### Ed Viesturs

# ED VIESTURS

is a world-renowned, preeminent, American high-altitude mountaineer who has climbed all 14 of the world's 8,000+ meter mountain peaks without oxygen. These peaks are above what is considered the "death zone," and Ed is only the fifth human to accomplish this feat without supplemental oxygen. Ed Viesturs has summited Mount Everest SEVEN Times!

# RISK-TAKING TIPS

## REJECT OUTSIDE PRESSURE

You'll likely make a lousy risk decision if you base it on the influence of outside pressure. Professional mountain climbers face pressure from many sources, including the media, equipment sponsors, paying clients, etc. "There's a huge difference between feeling that I have to do something and knowing what I should do. Feeling that you have to take a risk is usually a red flag that you've lost perspective and choice."

## INSTINCT MATTERS

When facing danger, your inner wisdom is the best guide. "Whether I climb or don't climb often comes down to instinct. If something doesn't feel right at the gut level, I won't do it. I've learned to trust that instinct."

## HAVE THE COURAGE TO SAY NO

The closer you get to the summit, the greater the temptation to keep climbing. The ambition of hungry "yes" can cloud one's judgment. "It takes courage to stop in your tracks and climb back down the mountain before reaching the summit. But because conditions change rapidly up there, sometimes walking back down is the choice that will keep you alive."

"

## GETTING TO THE TOP IS OPTIONAL. GETTING DOWN IS MANDATORY.

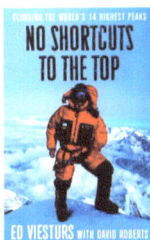

— ED VIESTURS
*No Shortcuts to the Top: Climbing the World's 14 Highest Peaks*

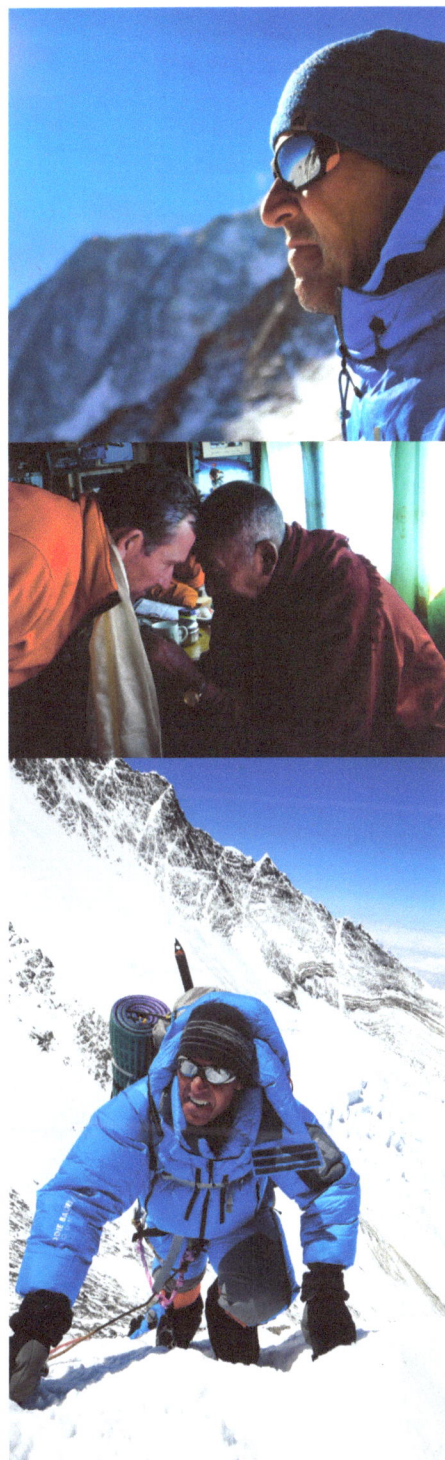

# RISK-TAKING:
## REFLECTIVE EVALUATION

**WHAT WILL YOU REGRET THE LEAST, TAKING THE RISK AND MAYBE FAILING?**
*Or not taking the risk and having to live with not knowing whether you would have been successful?*

**HAVING READ THE ENTIRE RISK-TAKING SECTION, YES OR NO, WILL YOU TAKE THE RISK?**
*If "yes," what are the first steps you can start taking within the next two weeks?*

Every decision involves two risks: the risk of action and the risk of inaction.
Relative to the last big decision you made, what were the risks of each?

| THE RISK OF ACTION | THE RISK OF INACTION |
|---|---|
| **WHAT ACTIONS DID YOU TAKE TO MANAGE THE RISK OF ACTION?** | **WHAT ACTIONS DID YOU TAKE TO MANAGE THE RISK OF INACTION?** |

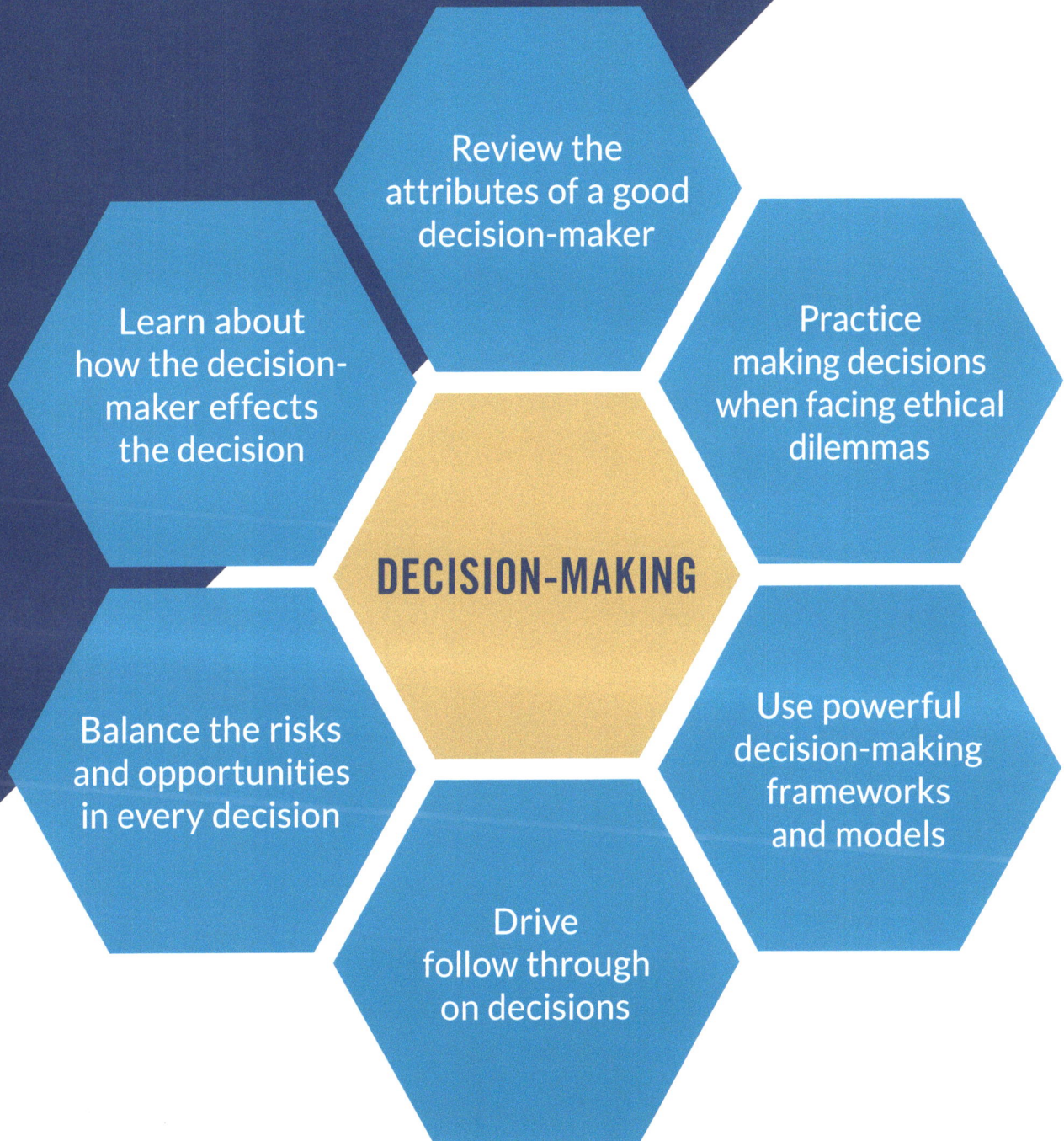

# OBJECTIVES

**DECISION-MAKING**

Review the attributes of a good decision-maker

Learn about how the decision-maker effects the decision

Practice making decisions when facing ethical dilemmas

Balance the risks and opportunities in every decision

Use powerful decision-making frameworks and models

Drive follow through on decisions

# REFLECTION QUESTIONS

WHAT ARE THE MAIN DECISIONS YOU MAKE IN A TYPICAL DAY AT WORK?

WHAT WAS THE BEST DECISION YOU EVER MADE, PERSONALLY AND PROFESSIONALLY?

WHAT WAS THE WORST DECISION YOU EVER MADE PERSONALLY AND PROFESSIONALLY?

# ATTRIBUTES OF A GOOD DECISION-MAKER

## ETHICAL
Ethical and Focused on "doing the right thing

## EMOTIONAL
Emotionally aware and can depersonalize

## INQUISITIVE
Asks great questions that clarify the problem or uncover assumptions

## APPROACHABLE
Gather other perspectives

## TOLERANCE
Are aware of their biases

## UNPRETENTIOUS
Keep their ego out of it

## BALANCED
Balanced multiple factors (balance heart and mind)

## CURIOUS
Always seek to learn after each decision is made

| WHAT ATTRIBUTES WOULD YOU ADD? | WHAT ATTRIBUTES DO YOU LACK? |
|---|---|
| | |

| ✔ DECIDING TRUMPS DELAYING WHEN: | ✘ DELAYING TRUMPS DECIDING WHEN: |
|---|---|
| • Safety could become jeopardized<br>• Delaying will cause the situation to get worse or larger<br>• Waiting will be too costly on finances or relationships | • There's more confusion than clarity<br>• Data about the issue is too conflicting<br>• Commitment from senior executives or the team to actually implement recommended action is too low |

# NINE DOT ACTIVITY

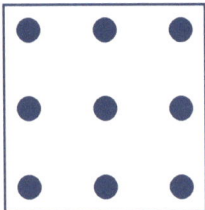

Place your pen down on one of the dots and draw four straight lines connecting all the dots, without lifting your pen off the paper, and without folding, mutilating or destroying the paper.

*See page 51 for answer.*

## BOUNDED RATIONALITY

We like to believe that we'll make **LOGICAL, FACTUAL, AND RATIONAL** decisions after weighing various factors and variable. However, as Nobel laureate Herbert Simon proposed, our own rationality is limited by the available information we're weighing, the time we have to make the decision, and the cognitive limitations of our own minds. We are bounded by our own rationality. Put another way, our irrationality often hurts our ability to make good decisions.

Because we lack perfect information, unlimited time, and supreme intelligence, we must make less-than-perfect choices—what Simon called **"SATISFICING BEHAVIOR."** The word combines "satisfy" with "suffice" and basically means we do the best we can with what we've got!

> "If we accept the proposition that both the knowledge and the computational power of the decision maker are severely limited, then we must distinguish between the real world and the actor's perception of it and reasoning about it."
> —*Herbert A. Simon*

# MR. LEMONFACE AND THE POWER OF IGNORANCE

In 1995 McArthur Wheeler rubbed lemon juice all over his face and robbed a bank. Later that same day he robbed another bank using the same trick.

It turns out that lemon juice has an interesting property. It can be used as invisible ink. If you use lemon juice to write a secret message, the letters only become revealed when exposed to heat. Mr. Wheeler assumed that it he rubbed lemon juice all over his face, his face would become invisible to the banks' security cameras. He had even tested it by taking a selfie with a Polaroid camera (which, evidently, he used incorrectly).

A few hours of the heists, the police got the surveillance tapes and had the local TV stations play them on the 11 O'clock news. Within an hour, Mr. Wheeler was identified as the bank robber. Later, when asked why he thought he could get away with the crime, Mr. Wheeler explained that it was the magical properties of lemon juice. He thought, wrongly, that the lemon juice would make him invisible.

Drawing on Mr. Wheeler's story for inspiration, two psychologists from Cornell University, David Dunning and Justin Kruger, decided to conduct a series of experiments to test how ignorance impacts decision-making. After being shown their test scores on assessments of logical reasoning, grammar skills, and humor, students were asked to estimate their own rank in the class. It turned out, the more incompetent a student was, the higher the assumed their rank would be. The converse was also true, the more ability a student had, the more they underestimated their competence. They would also assume that other as competent, if not more so, then themselves.

**THE DUNNING-KRUGER EFFECT SUGGESTS THAT THE GREATER YOUR IGNORANCE, THE MORE LIKELY YOU ARE TO:**

not recognize your lack of skill

lack awareness about the extent of your inadequacy

fail to accurately assess the skills of others

recognize and acknowledge your lack of skill only after getting training for that skill

*Excerpted from page 36 of A Leadership Kick in the Ass: How to Learn from Rough Landings, Blunders, and Missteps. By Bill Treasurer.*

# REFLECTION QUESTIONS

WHAT IMPLICATIONS DOES THE DUNNING-KRUGER EFFECT HAVE ON DECISION-MAKING?

RECALL THE LAST BIG DECISION YOU HAD TO MAKE. *What prominent factors drove the decision? Why was the decision important? What criteria did you use to make the decision? What was the outcome?*

# ETHICAL DILEMMAS

**(1)** A drunk competitor approaches you at an industry event and confides that he hates his company and is planning on quitting. You've known him for a long time and are surprised when he tells you that he just downloaded a bunch of files about the company's new strategy and proprietary new innovation. He tells you that he mailed the files to you today, and that all he asks is that you put in a good word for him when he approaches your company for a job.

**WHAT DO YOU DO?**

**(2)** You learn that one of your employees has been inputting faulty timecard data about his wife's arrival time to work each day (she is also an employee). When you confront the employee, he explains that they have a newborn baby at home and his wife can't leave for work until he gets home.

**WHAT DO YOU DO?**

**3**

You are an accountant in one of the company's must successful business units. The business unit leader hands you some receipts and asks you to reimburse him for $150 for the expenses he incurred while entertaining a client last night. Later, during lunch, you overhear the business unit lead laughing with his girlfriend about the great time the two of them had eating and dancing last night.

**WHAT DO YOU DO?**

**4**

Your company has a "no gift" policy, but you know of a few instances where people skirted around it. One of your subcontractors, whom you consider an old friend, sends you and your wife vouchers for an all-expense paid trip to Punta Cana. His note says, "Shhh, our secret!"

**WHAT DO YOU DO?**

Spanish runner Ivan Fernandez Anaya was competing in an international cross-country race and was in second place behind Kenyan runner, Abel Mutai. As they headed toward the home stretch, Mutai slowed down and stopped thinking he had already crossed the finish line.

Now, imagine that you're Anaya. You could easily pass Mutai and win the race. That's the whole goal of racing, right? What would you do?

Instead, Anaya came up to Mutai (the bronze medalist in the London Olympics) and pointed in the direction of the finish line, letting him know that he still had distance to cover. He later explained, "I didn't deserve to win it. I did what I had to do. He was the rightful winner. He created a gap that I couldn't have closed if he hadn't made the mistake. As soon as I saw him stopping, I knew I wasn't going to pass him."

## WHAT DOES THIS STORY TELL YOU ABOUT IVAN FERNANDEZ ANAYA'S VALUES?

## WHAT ARE YOUR TOP THREE DEEPEST-HELD VALUES, AND HOW DO THEY IMPACT THE WAY YOU MAKE DECISIONS

# GOOD DECISION FRAMEWORKS:

- Visually depict the important variables impacting the decision.
- Organize various thoughts and ideas.
- Reduce chaos, to the extent possible.
- Simplify the decision to its essential factors.
- Are useful in increasing the possibility of a successful outcome.

## THE PERSONAL PERFORMANCE MODEL

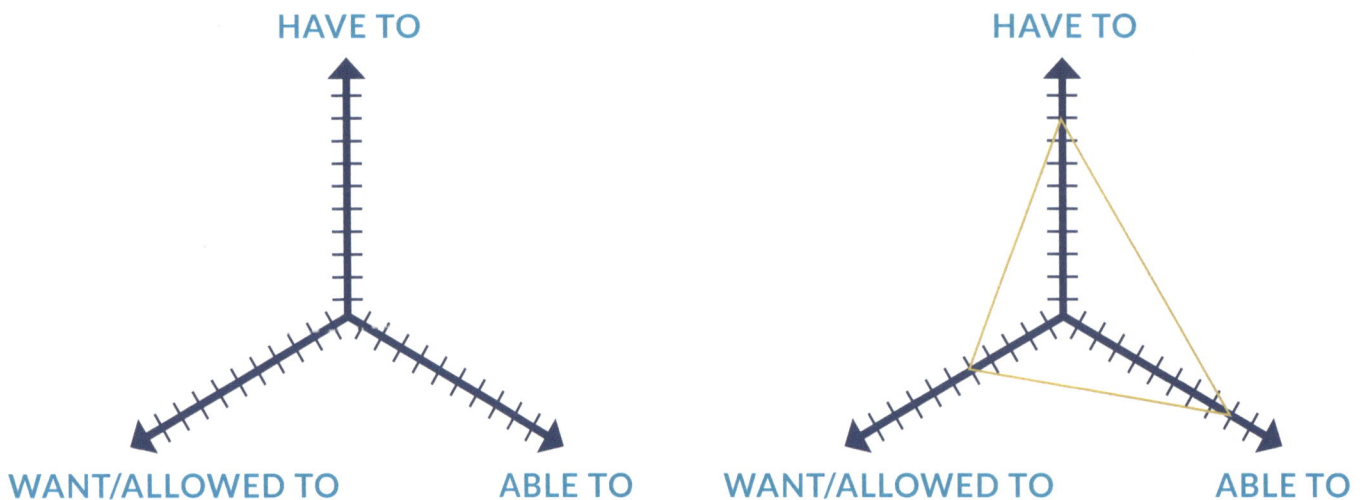

HAVE TO

WANT/ALLOWED TO · ABLE TO

HAVE TO

WANT/ALLOWED TO · ABLE TO

To use the Personal Performance Model, rate each category (three of them) on a scale of 0 – 10.

### HAVE TO:
To what extend are the tasks associate with your job imposed on you (i.e., you have to do them).

### ABLE TO:
To what extent is there a match between the tasks of your job and your abilities/skills?

### WANT TO:
To what extent do the tasks associated with your job correspond to what you really want to do?

Every few weeks reassess the graph. If the graphs are consistently low and/or never changing, you should ask yourself:

## WHAT DO I REALLY WANT?

## AM I EQUIPPED TO DO WHAT I REALLY WANT?

## DO I WANT WHAT I AM ACTUALLY ABLE TO DO?

## WHAT WILL IT TAKE TO GET WHAT I WANT?

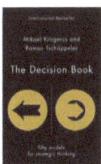

*The Personal Performance Model was introduced in* The Decision Book *by Mikael Krogerus and Roman Tschappeler.*

# THE SEVEN "S" MODEL

McKinsey is one of the most successful strategy consulting companies in the world. The "SEVEN 'S' MODEL" reflects the full complement of factors that leaders need to consider when making enterprise-wide decisions. The model is often used to identify gaps that might be creating imbalance, while also identifying improvement opportunities.

### STRATEGY
The overall plan for establishing competitive advantage and differentiation in the marketplace.

### STRUCTURE
The reporting structure that supports the strategy, and identify who reports to whom.

### SYSTEMS
Processes, systems, and activities that create efficiency so that people can do their work effectively.

### SHARED VALUES
Core values of the culture that make up the organization's identity, and guide behavior.

### STYLE
The leadership style that leaders and managers emulate.

### STAFF
The types of employees and the capabilities they provide to the organization.

### SKILLS
The competencies and skills that employees need to succeed in their roles for the organization.

# REFLECTION QUESTIONS

As you consider your big decision, run it through the Seven S Model to ensure that your thinking about it from multiple angles.

**STRATEGY:** *How will the decision differentiate you or further your long-term goals?*

**STRUCTURE:** *How will the decision impact the current organizational structure in your organization?*

**SYSTEMS:** *What will the impacts (+ & -) be on the organizational systems and processes?*

**SHARED VALUES:** *To what extent is the decision aligned with the organization's core values and mission?*

**STYLE:** *How will the decision impact how leaders lead in your organization?*

**STAFF:** *How is the decision likely to impact employees? What might the staffing / hiring implications be?*

**SKILLS:** *What competencies or skills will need to be developed as a result of the decision?*

# THE "WHAT DECISION METHOD"

Giant Leap Consulting developed the "What Decision Method" as part of it's risk-taking and decision-making workshop. To use the model, start under the "What?" heading, by evaluating the current circumstances surrounding the decision. Then work clockwise around the model answering each question along the way.

## HOW WHAT?
What metrics will you use to monitor the results of your decision?

## NOW WHAT?
What actions you will take that stem from your selected option?

## WHICH WHAT?
Which option is most likely to produce the outcome you desire? What's your choice?

## WHAT?
What is the condition with which you're starting?

## SO WHAT?
If the situation is left unaddressed, what will be the impacts?

## WHAT'S WHAT?
What options and alternatives do you have with which to address the situation?

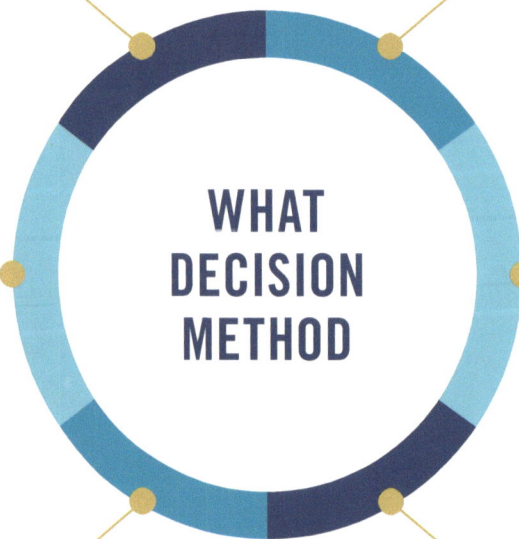

**WHAT DECISION METHOD**

"Here's a crazy question to ask when you're stuck trying to decide among two big choices; if you would die if you didn't make the choice right now, what choice would you make?"
—*Bill Treasurer, author,* Right Risk

# USING THE WHAT DECISION MODEL

Imagine that you are a member of the senior executive team of a $500 million-dollar manufacturing company. The CEO quickly organizes a meeting after conferencing with the board of directors. "We need to double the size of our business within 5 years. You need to get me some recommendations fast."

**USE THE "WHAT DECISION" MODEL TO MEET THE CEO'S REQUEST.**

| WHAT? | SO WHAT? |
|---|---|
| | |
| **WHAT'S WHAT?** | **WHICH WHAT?** |
| | |
| **NOW WHAT?** | **HOW WHAT?** |
| | |

# TRIANGULATION

Triangulation involves using multiple approaches to evaluate a decision or situation.

### QUESTION: "HOW LONG WILL IT TAKE TO COMPLETE THIS PROJECT?"

This question involves a prediction about the future, and since you can't be 100% certain about how the future will actually unfold, it's in your best interest to evaluate the question from multiple vantage points. This is the idea behind "Triangulation."

You could, for example, use a bottom-up approach, calculating the time task-by-task and seeing how they tally up. That gives you one answer. But another answer might come from evaluating the team's actual performance in meeting prior deadlines and milestones. If it consistently meets initial estimates, your answer would have a higher degree of confidence. You could also assess the question by comparing projects of similar size, scope, and complexity.

Triangulated decisions generally have more decision integrity than non-triangulated decisions because they are evaluated more rigorously and thoughtfully.

---

**TRIANGULATE THIS QUESTION:** *"How can we reduce our overhead costs?"*

---

"If all the estimates point to the same result, then you generate confidence in the answer."
—*Michael Kallet, author,* Think Smarter

# THE "WHY WHY" DIAGRAM

Often what first looks like a solution is really just a symptom of a deeper problem. Sometimes you have to look beyond the surface to really understand the causes of a problem. The "Why Why" diagram is derived from the work of Sakichi Toyoda of the Toyota Motor Corporation. He suggested that when facing a complex problem, and when trying to understand the true causes of a problem, it's important to keep asking "Why?" until you find the root causes, or until you say "I don't know." Once you say that, you've gotten to the item you need to work on to get more knowledge (the item you need to "know").

Imagine, for example, you work in a business that wins work based on being the lowest bidder. Over the last year, your company has lost bids to your competitors above your company's historical averages. The "Why Why" diagram might look like this...

| LOST BIDS | HIGH ESTIMATES | INADEQUATE INFO | POOR SYSTEMS |
| | LOWBALL COMPETITORS | ERRORS | LACK OF TIME TO RESEARCH |
| | | TOLERANCE FOR LOW MARGINS | LACK OF TRAINING |
| | | EFFICIENCIES | UPGRADED SYSTEMS |
| | | | STREAMLINED PROCESS |

# THE "HOW HOW" DIAGRAM

You can also create a "How How" diagram, depicting how you would go about solving a problem. In the space below, draw a How How diagram to think through ideas for sharply improving your company's productivity.

**DRAW A "HOW HOW" DIAGRAM**

# FORCE FIELD ANALYSIS

Kurt Lewin is considered the father of organizational development. Lewin taught at Stanford, Harvard, Cornell, and MIT, and his ideas about group dynamics, authority and power, and experiential learning are still being taught today.

Lewin also conducted applied research for the OSS (Office of Special Services—predecessor to the CIA). While there, he studied troop morale, advanced the idea of psychological warfare, and assisted with spy selection. Lewin believed that human behavior is a function of the interaction between a person and his/her environment. In other words, behavior is partly determined by a person's personality, and partly determined by the social situation they find themselves in.

Lewin believed that "forces" either drive or restrain change. If the forces promoting and inhibiting change are equal, there is "quasi-static equilibrium." However, when one force dominates over the other, change occurs. The box below depicts some of the driving and restraining forces that were at work before seatbelt laws were enacted.

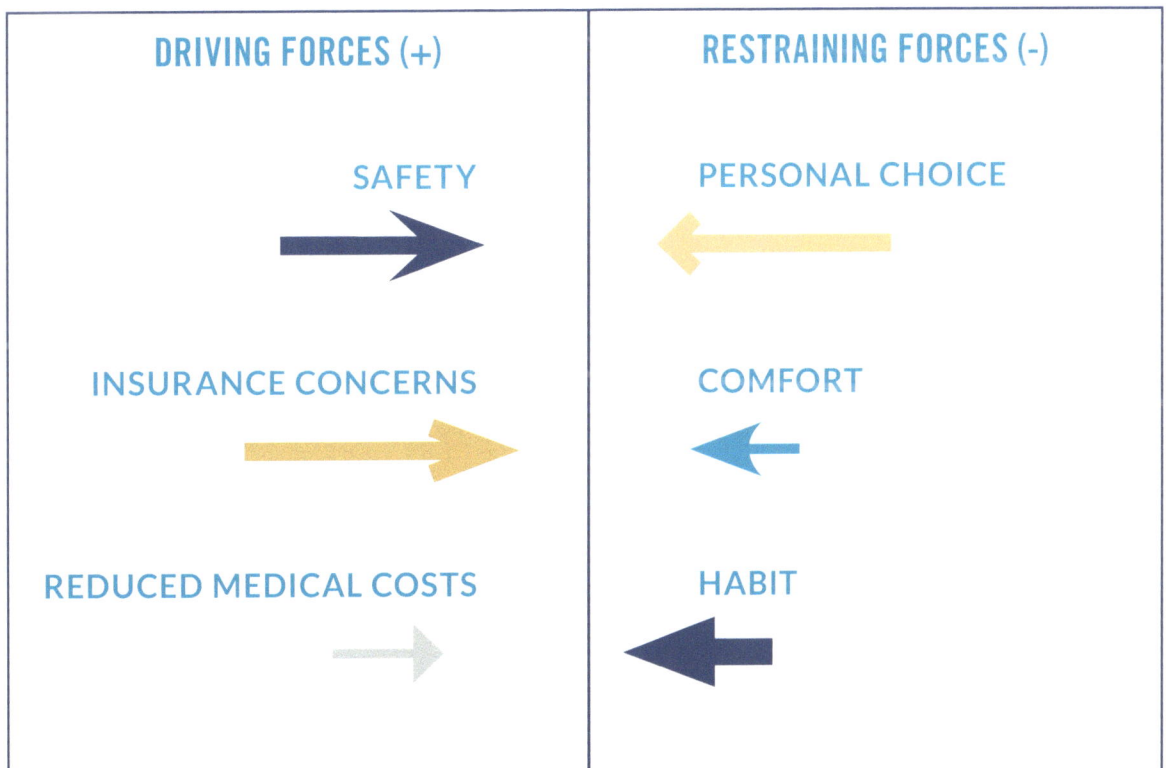

| DRIVING FORCES (+) | RESTRAINING FORCES (-) |
|---|---|
| SAFETY | PERSONAL CHOICE |
| INSURANCE CONCERNS | COMFORT |
| REDUCED MEDICAL COSTS | HABIT |

# FORCE FIELD ANALYSIS STEPS

1. Identify the current situation and desired future state

2. Identify what will occur if no action is taken

3. List the current driving and restraining forces

4. Draw an arrow to signify the strength of each driving and restraining force

5. Identify actions for increasing the strength of driving forces and reducing the strength of restraining forces (preferred)

## FORCE FIELD ANALYSIS: VARIATION

You can use a Sailboat/Ship metaphor to help explain driving and restraining forces. The ship represents the journey to a new destination.

- First, brainstorm the "WINDS" that are propelling the ship forward. These can be favorable "trade winds" or they could be "gale-force storm winds."

- Next, brainstorm the "ANCHORS"—what's holding us back from making this change. These are often internal to the organization and can include specific resistance, perceptions, lack of awareness, or a lack of tools.

- Then, brainstorm the "ROCKS"—these are the future obstacles that we need to avoid as we continue the journey.

- Finally, create your "VOYAGE PLAN" by determining actions to "harness the winds, let go of the anchors, and steer clear of the rocks."

- Use Post-it Notes to capture ideas for each portion of brainstorming. See AFFINITY DIAGRAM for more detail on using Post-It Notes.

- Bon voyage!

# THE DECISION TREE

Effective frameworks help break down complex situations into manageable chunks. Decisions are made easier to comprehend and manage when the piece parts that make up the decision can be graphically displayed. THE DECISION TREE is a type of diagram that allows you and your team to map out the various elements of a decision. They allow you to lay out various options so you can anticipate the outcomes that will likely emerge for each alternative option.

It's best to use THE DECISION TREE when working with a small team.

1. Working left to right, start with the decision that needs to be made.

2. Next, put the top viable options.

3. Finally, include the impacts the option is likely to produce.

**DECISION:**
- BUILD SOFTWARE
- BUY SOFTWARE
- ENHANCE WITH LEGACY SOFTWARE

**BUY COST: $800,000**

- SUCCESSFUL DEPLOYMENT: NO IMPACT
- UNSUCCESSFUL DEPLOYMENT: LOSS OF $2 MILLION

**BUILD COST: $500,000**

- SUCCESSFUL DEPLOYMENT: NO IMPACT
- UNSUCCESSFUL DEPLOYMENT: LOSS OF $2 MILLION

**ENHANCE COST: $150,000**

- SUCCESSFUL DEPLOYMENT: LOSS OF $2 MILLION

THE DECISION TREE can also be used to breakdown a large goal into detailed actions that can further the goal. Start by choosing a goal, such as "increase workplace morale". Next, generate the various means by which the goal could be achieved. Next, break each mean down into smaller options by asking, "How would this be addressed?" Repeat this question for each successive level of detail. Once you get to a task-level of detail, or the team exhausts all the possibilities, the Tree is complete. (Most times are done at three levels of detail).

| GOAL: INCREASE MORAL | | |
|---|---|---|
| | PROVIDE TRAINING | DEFINE NEEDS |
| | | SET CURRICULUM |
| | | SET BUDGET |
| | START A MENTORING PROGRAM | IDENTIFY MENTORS |
| | | IDENTIFY MENTEES |
| | | SET BUDGET |
| | GIVE EVERYONE A RAISE | ESTABLISH COSTS |
| | | GET EXEC APPROVAL |

**CREATE A DECISION TREE FOR INCREASING ORGANIZATIONAL COMMUNICATION IN YOUR COMPANY.**

# RACI CHART

A RACI Chart is used after a decision has been made to pinpoint what should be done by whom as a result of the decision.

**RESPONSIBLE:** The person or persons who will actually carry out the tasks.

**ACCOUNTABLE:** The person who assigns the work. Also the last person to review the assignment before it is deemed complete. There should only be one accountable person for each assignment.

**CONSULTED:** Subject matter experts or others whose impact or insights can be used to carry out the task. Oftentimes it is the people who will be impacted by the work.

**INFORMED:** Those who would benefit by being kept periodically informed about the progress of the assignment.

## TO CREATE THE CHART, USE THE FOLLOWING STEPS:

- List all the change related processes and/or activities
- Identify all of the roles and list them along the top
- Fill in the chart with the appropriate letters (R,A,C,I) for that task and person
- Ideally, there should only be one "A" or "R" per activity
  (too many for the same activity may indicate role confusion)
- Boxes with too many letters may need more clarification
- Activities with no "R" may be a problem

# SAMPLE ILLUSTRATION

|  | COMPANY EXEC TEAM MEMBER | DIVISION LEAD | SENIOR PROJECT MANAGER | SUPERVISOR |
|---|---|---|---|---|
| Activity 1 |  |  |  |  |
| Activity 2 |  |  |  |  |
| Activity 3 |  |  |  |  |
| Activity 4 |  |  |  |  |

**THINK ABOUT A MAJOR DECISION THAT YOU OR YOUR ORGANIZATION IS CONSIDERING.**
*Create a RACI chart based on what you already know.*

# "

**PEOPLE ATTAIN WORTH AND DIGNITY BY THE MULTITUDE OF DECISIONS THEY MAKE FROM DAY BY DAY.**

**THESE DECISIONS REQUIRE COURAGE.**

— ROLLO MAY
*Author of* The Courage to Create

# NINE DOT ACTIVITY ANSWER

*Activity on page 29*

## DEAR CLIENTS AND FRIENDS,

You are the focus of everything we do at Giant Leap Consulting. When you leave a Giant Leap workshop, seminar or keynote, you will be armed with practical strategies and tools that you can immediately put to use back at work. As I often tell our clients, the person leaving our training programs should not be the same person who entered it. You deserve to be more confident, skilled and capable after experiencing a Giant Leap program.

Since our founding in 2002, Giant Leap has been fortunate to have worked with thousands of executives from some of the best organizations in the world. You've taught us a lot about what works—and what doesn't—when it comes to adult learners. You can count on us to always provide learning experiences that have rich content, insightful dialogue, engaging activities, and relevant case studies.

There's something else you can count on too: first-rate course materials. Our participant notebooks, PowerPoints, and course materials are among the best in the world. I know that's a tall claim, but it's true! You can sample our course material and see for yourself!—just send an email to info@giantleapconsulting.com.

Please take a moment to immerse yourself in Giant Leap's new course catalogue. In addition to introducing our tried-and-true training courses, it also showcases our two "signature" programs: Courageous Leadership, and Open-door Leadership.

Stay Courageous!

*Bill Treasurer*

**BILL TREASURER**
Founder, Giant Leap Consulting, Inc.
*(GiantLeapConsulting.com)*

*P.S. Need a customized course? Giant Leap loves to develop new and original content for our clients!*
*Contact: info@giantleapconsulting.com*

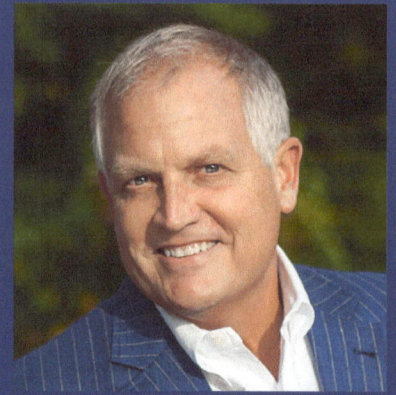

## ABOUT BILL'S KEYNOTES

In the past two decades, thousands of executives across the globe have attended Bill's keynotes and workshops. Benefiting from the concepts first introduced in Bill's bestselling books, participants come away with stronger leadership skills, improved team performance, and more career backbone.

Among others, Bill has led workshops for NASA, Accenture, Lenovo, USB Bank, CNN, Hugo Boss, SPANX, the Centers for Disease Control and Prevention, the U.S. Department of Veterans Affairs, and the Pittsburgh Pirates.

Bill's insights about courage and risk-taking have been featured in over 100 newspapers and magazines, including the Washington Post, NY Daily News, Chicago Tribune, Atlanta Journal Constitution, Boston Herald, Woman's Day, Redbook, Fitness, and The Harvard Management Update.

**VISIT OUR WEBSITES:**
giantleapconsulting.com
billtreasurer.com

Little Leaps Press, Inc.
2 Lynwood Road
Asheville, NC 28804

Bulk Order Sales: Special discounts may be available for large quantity sales. For details, call: 800-867-7239.

Title: Coaching Excellence, Elevating Performance Through Coaching
Author: Bill Treasurer
Publication Date: June 1, 2019
Publisher: Little Leaps Press, Inc.

Published in the United States of America
by Little Leaps Press, Inc.
ISBN: 978-1-948058-26-1

LITTLE LEAPS
PRESS

www.ingramcontent.com/pod-product-compliance
Lightning Source LLC
Chambersburg PA
CBHW041704200326
41518CB00003B/188